THE OFFICIAL NFL ANNUAL 2016

Written by Neil Reynolds

Designed by Bradley Scott-Peterson

A Grange Publication

©2015. Published by Grange Communications Ltd., Edinburgh, under licence from NFL Properties LLC. Printed in the EU.

Photographs © AP Images, Dave Shopland, Sean Ryan, Action Images and Shutterstock.

ISBN 978-1-910199-61-9

3

CONTENTS

THIS IS THE NFL!

Welcome to the fast-paced, action-packed world of the NFL where some of the greatest athletes on the planet will wow you with their amazing displays of skill, speed and strength.

Maybe it's the running back rumbling down the field, tacklers pinging off him like hailstones, or the football flying 60 yards in the air to a speeding receiver. It could be the menace of a linebacker chasing down the quarterback in order to deliver a big hit, or a lightning-quick cornerback batting away a would-be touchdown pass.

Whatever the attraction, the NFL is America's number one passion and is as much a part of the country's culture as the stars and stripes flag and home-made apple pie.

But the NFL is no longer just America's favourite sporting headline act – regular season games are now played in London every year as the United Kingdom stakes a serious claim to a potential team of its own in the future.

NFL American football games are a full-on experience complete with awe-inspiring fly-overs, cheerleader performances and music acts and when each dramatic contest is played out on the gridiron, fans around the world find themselves glued to thrilling action full of intrigue and tactics.

And one of the best things about the NFL is that you never quite know what is going to happen. The league prides itself on being one of the most wide-open in any professional sport. Over the last 10 seasons, the NFL has produced eight different Super Bowl champions and surprise results are regular features of every excitement-filled weekend.

Now is the perfect time to be an NFL fan because an offensive explosion means high-scoring games and dramatic finishes are the norm. Scoring and offensive production is at an all-time high and more than half of all games are decided by a single score, meaning your fingernails may not make it to the end of some thrilling contests.

But if those kind of statistics are not your thing, the players of the NFL will still demand your attention. Tune in on any given Sunday and you'll see a stunning mix of speed, athleticism and raw power.

You will not be disappointed. Enjoy!

Linebacker

"Linebackers are the biggest hitters on the team. We have to be able to stop the running back but also cover potential passing targets downfield."
– *San Francisco 49ers linebacker Navorro Bowman.*

Cornerback

"The primary role of a cornerback is to mark the wide receiver on passing plays – we're like the receiver's shadow and can also catch the ball."
– *New York Jets cornerback Darrelle Revis.*

Safety

"The safety is the last line of defence. We need to defend deep balls thrown downfield but we also come closer to the line and make tackles."
– *Minnesota Vikings safety Harrison Smith.*

MEET THE TEAMS: AFC EAST

It's time to meet the 32 teams that make up the NFL, starting with the AFC East Division...

BUFFALO BILLS

FORMED:	1960
STADIUM:	Ralph Wilson Stadium
HEAD COACH:	Rex Ryan

Feeding off the emotion and excitement of their head coach, Rex Ryan, the Bills are a confident team on the rise who lean on one of the best defences in the NFL. They are backed by loud and passionate fans desperate for success.

STAR MAN – LeSEAN McCOY, RUNNING BACK. McCoy is an elusive runner who can score from anywhere on the field. He put his explosive skills to good use in 2013 when he led the NFL in rushing. The Bills acquired him in a trade with Philadelphia in 2015.

DID YOU KNOW?
The Bills lost an NFL record four Super Bowls in a row from 1990-1993.

MIAMI DOLPHINS

FORMED:	1966
STADIUM:	Sun Life Stadium
HEAD COACH:	Joe Philbin

The Dolphins are one of the most popular teams among British NFL fans, dating back to the days of the great Dan Marino. With quarterback Ryan Tannehill at the helm, the Dolphins boast a young squad looking for a playoff return.

STAR MAN – NDAMUKONG SUH, DEFENSIVE TACKLE. He's big, he's bad and he makes life a misery for opposing quarterbacks. Suh is one of the NFL's best defenders and became the highest-paid (six years, $114 million) when he joined Miami in 2015.

DID YOU KNOW?
The Dolphins have played three regular season games in London in 2007, 2014 and 2015.

NEW ENGLAND PATRIOTS

FORMED:	1966
STADIUM:	Gillette Stadium
HEAD COACH:	Bill Belichick

The Patriots have set the gold standard in terms of recent NFL success and are the team everyone wants to catch. The defending Super Bowl champions have played in six of the last 14 title games, emerging as champions four times.

STAR MAN – TOM BRADY, QUARTERBACK. Tom Brady is the most successful quarterback in NFL history. He has played in six Super Bowls with the Patriots and has won a record-tying four league titles. Quite simply, Brady is an all-time legend.

DID YOU KNOW?
Brady was the 199th player chosen in the 2000 NFL Draft. Six quarterbacks were taken before him.

NEW YORK JETS

FORMED:	1966
STADIUM:	MetLife Stadium
HEAD COACH:	Todd Bowles

The Jets have a tradition of producing some of the stronger defences in the NFL and they are now adding weapons to their attack to become a more rounded team and a playoff contender.

STAR MAN – DARRELLE REVIS, CORNERBACK. Revis is the one of the NFL's best and has made a small fortune shadowing wide receivers. He began his career with the Jets and, after spells with Tampa Bay and New England, returned home in 2015.

DID YOU KNOW?
The Jets' lone Super Bowl success came in the 1968 season when they were led by colourful and controversial quarterback Joe Namath.

BALTIMORE RAVENS

FORMED: 1996

STADIUM: M&T Bank Stadium

HEAD COACH: John Harbaugh

The Ravens are a well-run, well-built and physical team who just know how to win. Led by quarterback Joe Flacco, Baltimore are always in contention and won the Super Bowl as recently as the 2012 season.

STAR MAN – JOE FLACCO, QUARTERBACK. At first glance, Flacco is quiet and pretty ordinary. But he is a fierce competitor who is at his best in the big playoff games. He was named Most Valuable Player of Baltimore's most recent Super Bowl win and that earned him a $120 million contract.

DID YOU KNOW?

The Ravens have been in existence for less than 20 years but already have two Super Bowl crowns (2000 and 2012 seasons).

CINCINNATI BENGALS

FORMED: 1968

STADIUM: Paul Brown Stadium

HEAD COACH: Marvin Lewis

The Bengals have been one of the NFL's more consistent teams, making the end-of-season playoffs in each of the last four years. They are led by a defensive-minded coach but actually possess considerable points-scoring talent on offense.

STAR MAN – A.J. GREEN – WIDE RECEIVER. Green is young, exciting and extremely productive. When he gets into full stride and uses his 6-foot-4 height, Green is hard to contain and has established himself as one of the league's most dangerous receivers.

DID YOU KNOW?

Quarterback Andy Dalton likes to practice yoga to stay in shape during the course of a season.

CLEVELAND BROWNS

FORMED: 1950

STADIUM: FirstEnergy Stadium

HEAD COACH: Mike Pettine

The Browns have a rich history that saw them win four league titles from 1950 to 1964. They are trying to recapture that former glory and 2014 saw them provide much excitement before a late slide knocked them from playoff contention.

STAR MAN – JOE HADEN, CORNERBACK. Haden has been a regular starter in Cleveland since joining the team as a first round draft pick in 2010. Haden has been voted an NFL All-Star in each of the past two seasons.

DID YOU KNOW?

The most committed Browns fans occupy an area of their stadium known as 'The Dawg Pound' and spend three hours each Sunday during the season dressed as dogs and barking like mad!

PITTSBURGH STEELERS

FORMED: 1933

STADIUM: Heinz Field

HEAD COACH: Mike Tomlin

The Steelers are the most successful team in the NFL's Super Bowl era, lifting the Vince Lombardi Trophy a record six times. Led by quarterback Ben Roethlisberger, Pittsburgh boast one of the NFL's best attacks and are regular playoff contenders.

STAR MAN – ANTONIO BROWN, WIDE RECEIVER. Brown started out as a kick returner and uses those elusive skills to frustrate defenders after the catch. And he makes a lot of catches! Brown led the NFL with 129 receptions in 2014.

DID YOU KNOW?

The Steelers only have their logo on one side of the helmets. This was introduced as an experiment in 1962 and because the team played well that season, it was never changed.

MEET THE TEAMS: AFC SOUTH

HOUSTON TEXANS

FORMED: 2002
STADIUM: NRG Stadium
HEAD COACH: Bill O'Brien

The Texans are the youngest franchise in the NFL having been formed in 2002 and have enjoyed some success in recent years, qualifying for the playoffs in 2011 and 2012. With a tough defence and a developing attack, Houston could be a club on the rise.

STAR MAN – J.J. WATT, DEFENSIVE END. There is not a more devastating defender in the NFL than J.J. Watt and he is the league's reigning Defensive Player of the Year. Watt has an incredible combination of strength and speed that makes him impossible to contain each weekend.

DID YOU KNOW?
The team's 'Texans' nickname came about following an online survey of more than 65,000 fans and was chosen ahead of Bobcats, Stallions, Toros and Apollos.

INDIANAPOLIS COLTS

FORMED: 1953
STADIUM: Lucas Oil Stadium
HEAD COACH: Chuck Pagano

The Colts are one of the most exciting teams to watch in the NFL and they are also one of the league's most consistently successful clubs, qualifying for the playoffs in 12 of the last 13 seasons. The Colts boasted the NFL's top-ranked passing attack in 2014 as they reached the Super Bowl semi-finals.

STAR MAN – ANDREW LUCK, QUARTERBACK. Luck replaced a living legend in Peyton Manning in 2012 and has handled that pressure with ease, leading the Colts to the playoffs every year since he's been in the league. With a strong and accurate arm and outstanding intelligence, Luck is already one of the top players in the NFL.

DID YOU KNOW?
Luck grew up in London and then Germany while his father, former NFL quarterback Oliver, served as president of the NFL Europe League.

JACKSONVILLE JAGUARS

FORMED: 1995
STADIUM: EverBank Field
HEAD COACH: Gus Bradley

The Jaguars may boast one of the youngest squads in the NFL but there is a buzz building around this team thanks to some outstanding off-season additions in 2015 and the excitable leadership skills of head coach Gus Bradley. The Jags are on the right track and are a team on the rise.

STAR MAN – JULIUS THOMAS, TIGHT END. This former basketball player is very hard to defend due to his combination of size and speed and has become one of the best tight ends in the NFL. The Jags spent big to sign him during the off-season.

DID YOU KNOW?
The Jaguars have agreed to play at least one regular season game in London from 2013-2016.

TENNESSEE TITANS

FORMED: 1960
STADIUM: The Nissan Stadium
HEAD COACH: Ken Whisenhunt

The Titans have fallen on hard times in recent years and have not made the playoffs since the 2008 season. But they have been aggressive in adding talented young players to their team and will be hoping to become contenders again in the near future.

STAR MAN – MARCUS MARIOTA, QUARTERBACK. The second player picked in the 2015 NFL Draft, Mariota offers hope for the future in Tennessee and has already become the face of the team. Mariota was named college football's best player in 2014.

DID YOU KNOW?
The Titans were originally the Houston Oilers until moving to Nashville in 1999 and changing their nickname.

MEET THE TEAMS: AFC WEST

DENVER BRONCOS

FORMED: 1960

STADIUM: Sports Authority Field at Mile High

HEAD COACH: Gary Kubiak

The Broncos boast one of the most exciting attacks in the NFL and have enjoyed considerable success, reaching the end-of-season playoffs for the past four years. The Broncos have played in seven Super Bowls, most recently during the 2013 season when they lost to Seattle.

STAR MAN – PEYTON MANNING, QUARTERBACK. While he may be coming towards the end of his Hall of Fame career, 39-year-old Manning remains one of the most productive and dangerous quarterbacks in the NFL. By the time he finally retires, Manning will own every meaningful passing record in the book.

DID YOU KNOW?
Manning has been voted to the Pro Bowl All-Star game 14 times during his career and owns more than 60 league records.

KANSAS CITY CHIEFS

FORMED: 1960

STADIUM: Arrowhead Stadium

HEAD COACH: Andy Reid

Backed by some of the loudest and most passionate fans in America, the Chiefs are a competitive team built around a strong running game and an aggressive and attacking defence.

STAR MAN – JUSTIN HOUSTON, OUTSIDE LINEBACKER. Houston is one of the most explosive and athletic defenders in the NFL. He uses his outstanding speed to close on opposing quarterbacks and can deliver quite a hit when he gets into the backfield.

DID YOU KNOW?
Chiefs fans officially became the loudest in world sport on September 29, 2014, when their roars reached 142.2 decibels (louder than a military jet on take-off) against the New England Patriots.

OAKLAND RAIDERS

FORMED: 1960

STADIUM: O.Co Coliseum

HEAD COACH: Jack Del Rio

The Raiders are one of the NFL's most colourful, controversial and best-supported teams. But these three-time Super Bowl winners are fighting to recapture their former glory having not qualified for the NFL playoffs since the 2002 season.

STAR MAN – KHALIL MACK, OUTSIDE LINEBACKER. At the beginning of each play, the explosive and energetic Mack flies into the opposing backfield as if he's been shot out of a cannon. The second-year player looks like being the leader of Oakland's defence for many years to come.

DID YOU KNOW?
The Raiders have a true Brit on their roster in the form of offensive tackle Menelik Watson, who was born and raised in Manchester.

SAN DIEGO CHARGERS

FORMED: 1960

STADIUM: Qualcomm Stadium

HEAD COACH: Mike McCoy

If you fancy combining some California sunshine with watching your favourite NFL club, the San Diego Chargers could be your team! Led by one of the top quarterbacks in the game in Philip Rivers, the Chargers are exciting to watch and are regular playoff contenders.

STAR MAN – PHILIP RIVERS, QUARTERBACK. Rivers is not the most athletic-looking quarterback in the NFL. But this fiery veteran launches accurate passes all over the field and refuses to be intimidated by even the toughest of NFL defenders.

DID YOU KNOW?
The Chargers played a regular season game at Wembley Stadium in 2008, losing a 37-32 thriller to the New Orleans Saints.

MEET THE TEAMS: NFC EAST

DALLAS COWBOYS

FORMED: 1960

STADIUM: AT&T Stadium

HEAD COACH: Jason Garrett

The Cowboys are arguably the NFL's most popular club and have long been labelled 'America's Team.' The boys from Texas – who boast an exciting offense - have played in a record eight Super Bowls, winning five league crowns.

STAR MAN – TONY ROMO, QUARTERBACK. Romo was the highest-rated quarterback in the NFL last season and is always exciting to watch. The four-time all-star can frustrate defenders with his speed and elusiveness before firing accurate passes downfield.

DID YOU KNOW?

Young players who join the Cowboys during each pre-season are not given a helmet with the famous star logo on each side until they have officially made the final 53-man roster. The stars are then added.

NEW YORK GIANTS

FORMED: 1925

STADIUM: MetLife Stadium

HEAD COACH: Tom Coughlin

The Giants are one of the oldest teams in the NFL and they are a club with a great history, winning eight league titles, including four in the Super Bowl era. The Giants most recently won Super Bowls at the end of the 2007 and 2011 seasons.

STAR MAN – ODELL BECKHAM JR., WIDE RECEIVER. With sprinter's speed and outstanding catching ability, Odell Beckham Jr is set to dominate the NFL for the next decade or more. He is already considered one of the most dangerous receivers in the sport.

DID YOU KNOW?

Giants quarterback Eli Manning is the younger brother of Denver Broncos quarterback Peyton Manning. Their father, Archie, was an NFL quarterback from 1971 to 1984.

PHILADELPHIA EAGLES

FORMED: 1933

STADIUM: Lincoln Financial Field

HEAD COACH: Chip Kelly

The Eagles play a fast-paced and exciting brand of American football that is hard to ignore. Led by a tactical genius in Chip Kelly, the Eagles can score points for fun and are competitive and entertaining each and every weekend.

STAR MAN – DeMARCO MURRAY, RUNNING BACK. Murray is one of the best running backs in the NFL and was the league's rushing champion last season. The multi-talented running back can bulldoze through would-be tacklers yet also has the speed to race away from defenders.

DID YOU KNOW?

When the Eagles officially opened Lincoln Financial Field in 2003, Sylvester Stallone – who played Philadelphia's own Rocky Balboa – was on hand to get the crowd fired up.

WASHINGTON REDSKINS

FORMED: 1932

STADIUM: FedEx Field

HEAD COACH: Jay Gruden

The Redskins are among the older teams in the NFL and boast a rich history, winning five league titles, including three Super Bowls. Cheered on by a passionate and vocal fan base, the Redskins are more popular than the politicians who work in their city!

STAR MAN – DeSEAN JACKSON, WIDE RECEIVER. With electrifying pace, DeSean Jackson is one of the most exciting players in the NFL and has the ability to take even the shortest of passes the length of the field for a touchdown. Jackson has an array of breath-taking moves and is a true star.

DID YOU KNOW?

Redskins quarterback Robert Griffin III is renowned for his extensive collection of bright and colourful socks and he even has his own range on sale in the United States.

MEET THE TEAMS: NFC NORTH

CHICAGO BEARS

FORMED: 1920

STADIUM: Soldier Field

HEAD COACH: John Fox

The Chicago Bears are one of the NFL's original teams dating back to 1920 and inaugural owner George Halas is considered one of the league's founding fathers. The Bears have a history of being a tough, no-nonsense team built in the image of their passionate fans.

STAR MAN – MATT FORTE, RUNNING BACK. Matt Forte is considered to be one of the top running backs in the NFL but he is much more than a one-dimensional runner for the Bears. In 2014, Forte became just the second player in league history to rush for 1,000 yards and catch 100 passes in the same season.

DID YOU KNOW?

The Bears have several players with footballing families. Guard Kyle Long's brother Chris is a defensive end for St. Louis, tight end Martellus Bennett's brother Michael is a defensive lineman for Seattle and cornerback Kyle Fuller's brother Corey is a wide receiver for Detroit.

MINNESOTA VIKINGS

FORMED: 1961

STADIUM: TFC Bank Stadium

HEAD COACH: Mike Zimmer

The Vikings have never won a Super Bowl (they are 0-4 in the big game) but they are considered to be a rising team under second-year head coach Mike Zimmer. With star running back Adrian Peterson joining young quarterback Teddy Bridgewater in the backfield, the Vikings' hopes are high.

STAR MAN – HARRISON SMITH, SAFETY. There are players on Minnesota's roster who get more newspaper headlines, but there are few as important to the team's success as hard-hitting safety Harrison Smith. The tough playmaker out of Notre Dame hits hard but also has the ball skills to make timely interceptions and is an unsung hero.

DID YOU KNOW?

Rookie linebacker Eric Kendricks is playing in the NFL with the Vikings even though he has only enjoyed five birthdays. But don't worry, the second round selection is not five years old. He was born in a leap year on February 29, 1992.

GREEN BAY PACKERS

FORMED: 1921

STADIUM: Lambeau Field

HEAD COACH: Mike McCarthy

The Packers are one of the most unique franchises in American sports as the fans own the team. Despite being a small-town team, the Packers have been giants on the field, winning an incredible 13 NFL titles. The modern-day Packers are free-scoring, talented and exciting to watch.

STAR MAN – AARON RODGERS, QUARTERBACK. Aaron Rodgers is deemed by many to be the best quarterback in the NFL today. He has already won a Super Bowl ring and guided Green Bay to the semi-finals last year. Statistically, the strong-armed and accurate Rodgers is tabbed as the highest-rated quarterback in NFL history.

DID YOU KNOW?

Packers players celebrate every touchdown at home games by jumping into the stands and celebrating with the fans. The move – known as The Lambeau Leap – draws a special exemption from the NFL's excessive celebration rule.

DETROIT LIONS

FORMED: 1930

STADIUM: Ford Field

HEAD COACH: Jim Caldwell

The Lions are one of the more exciting teams to watch in the NFL and will hope to advance deeper into the playoffs in 2015 after losing in the wild card round last term. The Lions – who are one of the league's oldest teams, are loaded with offensive talent and also boast a tough defence.

STAR MAN – CALVIN JOHNSON, WIDE RECEIVER. At 6-foot-5, Calvin Johnson is an imposing and dominant target who has grown to become arguably the best wide receiver in the NFL today and one of the all-time greats. Johnson is a physical mis-match for opposing defensive backs and an every-week star.

DID YOU KNOW?

Lions rookie offensive lineman Laken Tomlinson may just be starting his American football career but he already has plans for life after the NFL. The 2015 first round draft choice plans to become a brain surgeon.

MEET THE TEAMS: NFC SOUTH

ATLANTA FALCONS

FORMED: 1966

STADIUM: Georgia Dome

HEAD COACH: Dan Quinn

Behind star quarterback Matt Ryan and some exciting offensive talent, the Falcons came within one win of grabbing a playoff berth last season. But they needed to add some defensive muscle and are now looking to improve under the leadership of former Seahawks coordinator Dan Quinn.

STAR MAN – JULIO JONES, WIDE RECEIVER. Julio Jones is a big, strong and dominant wide receiver capable of becoming one of the very best in the business. When on top form, Jones is tough to defend and is a true star. He has broken the 1,000-yard receiving barrier in two of the last three seasons.

DID YOU KNOW?

Atlanta's first round draft pick in 2015, Clemson pass-rushing ace Vic Beasley, grew up in Adairsville, Georgia, and is a life-long Falcons fan. Beasley is expected to seriously upgrade the Falcons defence in the coming years.

CAROLINA PANTHERS

FORMED: 1995

STADIUM: Bank of America Stadium

HEAD COACH: Ron Rivera

Led by one of the toughest defences in the NFL, the Panthers won the NFC South Division in 2014, becoming the first team in that division to win back-to-back titles. With the defence in place, the Panthers are adding more offensive firepower and are ready to mount a Super Bowl challenge.

STAR MAN – CAM NEWTON, QUARTERBACK. The first overall pick in the 2011 NFL Draft recently inked a $100 million deal with the Panthers, cementing his status as the undisputed star on the team. Newton can shred defences with his strong arm but is equally at home running the ball and scoring touchdowns on the ground.

DID YOU KNOW?

Panthers head coach Ron Rivera is a former NFL linebacker who won a Super Bowl ring as a member of the 1985 Chicago Bears. Rivera played his entire career with the Bears from 1984 to 1992.

NEW ORLEANS SAINTS

FORMED: 1967

STADIUM: Mercedes-Benz Superdome

HEAD COACH: Sean Payton

If you like seeing plenty of points scored, the Saints could be the team for you. While the names can change from year to year, the offensive production of the Saints remains the same. They are exciting to watch and are regularly in the playoff race while being cheered on by their passionate fans.

STAR MAN – DREW BREES, QUARTERBACK. Even though 36-year-old Brees is inching towards the latter stages of his NFL career, the Saints have a playoff hope every time he steps onto the field. Brees is one of the smaller quarterbacks in the NFL at 6-foot, but he shines due to his outstanding accuracy and decision-making.

DID YOU KNOW?

Since Sean Payton took over as head coach and Drew Brees became the Saints quarterback in 2006, New Orleans have never ranked lower than sixth in total offense among the NFL's 32 teams.

TAMPA BAY BUCCANEERS

FORMED: 1976

STADIUM: Raymond James Stadium

HEAD COACH: Lovie Smith

The Buccaneers finished last season with the worst record in the NFL but there are hopes for a quick turnaround following the drafting of star rookie quarterback Jameis Winston. The Bucs are putting some exciting young attacking players in place and should be a team on the rise.

STAR MAN – GERALD McCOY, DEFENSIVE TACKLE. For a big man capable of dominating opponents physically with his strength, Gerald McCoy boasts cat-like quickness and continues to make life tough for quarterbacks around the NFL. McCoy routinely negotiates traffic along the line of scrimmage and makes big plays for the Bucs' defence.

DID YOU KNOW?

The Buccaneers have played two regular season games at Wembley Stadium, losing to the New England Patriots in 2009 and the Chicago Bears in 2011.

MEET THE TEAMS: NFC WEST

ARIZONA CARDINALS

FORMED: 1920

STADIUM: University of Phoenix Stadium

HEAD COACH: Bruce Arians

The Cardinals are one of the oldest teams in the NFL having been formed in 1920. More recently – under inspirational coach Bruce Arians – the Cardinals have adopted a gritty, never-say-die attitude that helped them reach the playoffs in 2014. They are now chasing their first league title since 1947.

STAR MAN – PATRICK PETERSON, CORNERBACK. With the speed and strength needed to match up with the best wide receivers around the league, Patrick Peterson is one of the game's elite cover defenders. He battled through diabetes early in 2014 but is now back to his very best and is a Cardinals star.

DID YOU KNOW?

Wide receiver Larry Fitzgerald likes to travel the world when he's not playing American football and has visited countries such as Russia and South Africa. On a trip to Asia, Fitzgerald ate monkey brains!

SAN FRANCISCO 49ERS

FORMED: 1946

STADIUM: Levi's Stadium

HEAD COACH: Jim Tomsula

The 49ers are one of the most successful teams in NFL history, winning five Super Bowls and appearing in the title game at the end of the 2012 season. Only the Pittsburgh Steelers have more Super Bowl wins than the Niners, who remain a tough and gritty squad built in the image of their coach.

STAR MAN – NaVORRO BOWMAN, LINEBACKER. Despite missing the entire 2014 season due to a serious knee injury, NaVorro Bowman is still widely considered among the very best defenders in the NFL and is an undisputed leader of a tough San Francisco defence. This tackling machine inspires those around him to play at a higher level.

DID YOU KNOW?

49ers head coach Jim Tomsula got his professional coaching break in London in 1998, where he served as defensive line coach for the England Monarchs. He also coached in Scotland and Germany before heading to the NFL.

SEATTLE SEAHAWKS

FORMED: 1976

STADIUM: CenturyLink Field

HEAD COACH: Pete Carroll

The Seattle Seahawks have been one of the most dominant NFL teams in recent years, reaching the last two Super Bowls and winning the championship after the 2013 campaign. The 'Hawks are brash, confident and aggressive and they're cheered on by some of the noisiest fans in world sport.

STAR MAN – MARSHAWN LYNCH, RUNNING BACK. When Marshawn Lynch begins running with fearsome power, fans around the league know he has entered 'Beast Mode.' This powerful, wrecking ball of a running back once scored on such a spectacular, tackle-breaking run that Seahawks fans set off a small earthquake in Seattle.

DID YOU KNOW?

Seahawks quarterback Russell Wilson is not only one of the best young American football stars in the NFL, he is also an accomplished baseball player. His baseball rights are held by the Texas Rangers.

ST. LOUIS RAMS

FORMED: 1936

STADIUM: Edward Jones Dome

HEAD COACH: Jeff Fisher

The Rams are a tough and dangerous team, capable of beating the very best the NFL has to offer on any given weekend. With a dominating defence and an improving attack, the Rams are considered to be a team on the rise who could be contending for honours soon.

STAR MAN – ROBERT QUINN, DEFENSIVE END. There are many technical reasons why Robert Quinn is one of the top defenders in the NFL but, above everything else, he is a relentless player who simply refuses to be blocked. Quinn is the leader of an aggressive Rams defence and a nightmare for opposing quarterbacks.

DID YOU KNOW?

Rams head coach Jeff Fisher played defensive back for the Chicago Bears team that won the Super Bowl at the end of the 1985 season.

AND THE WINNER IS...

American football is very much a team sport but individuals are still recognised for outstanding performances, and that was the case ahead of last season's Super Bowl in America. At the glitzy NFL Honours event in Phoenix, Arizona, the greatest performers of the 2014 season were rewarded for their all-round skills!

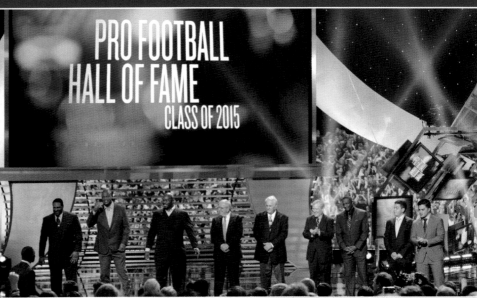

MOST VALUABLE PLAYER

Aaron Rodgers, Green Bay Packers quarterback Rodgers was named the top player in the NFL for the second time in his glittering career. The laser-armed passer remains the highest-rated quarterback in NFL history.

DEFENSIVE ROOKIE OF THE YEAR
Aaron Donald, St. Louis Rams defensive tackle

DEFENSIVE PLAYER OF THE YEAR

J.J. Watt, Houston Texans defensive end Watt turned in one of the most dominant defensive displays of all time. Not content with hitting NFL quarterbacks, the man mountain also made special appearances on offense and scored a total of five touchdowns.

COACH OF THE YEAR

Bruce Arians, Arizona Cardinals head coach Arians was named the NFL's top coach for the second time in the last three years. The Cardinals lost their top two quarterbacks to injury but still won 11 of 16 games and made the playoffs thanks to their inspirational coach.

OFFENSIVE PLAYER OF THE YEAR

DeMarco Murray, Dallas Cowboys running back Murray was an iron man who carried the Cowboys to the quarter-final stage of the NFL playoffs, leading the league with 1,845 yards and 13 scores on a bruising 392 runs. It was not enough to keep him in Dallas and he joined Philadelphia after the season.

COMEBACK PLAYER OF THE YEAR
Rob Gronkowski, New England Patriots tight end

OFFENSIVE ROOKIE OF THE YEAR
Odell Beckham Jr, New York Giants wide receiver.

NFL MAN OF THE YEAR
Thomas Davis, Carolina Panthers linebacker.

HOW THE SUPER BOWL WAS WON!

Last season's championship showdown - Super Bowl XLIX (49) between the Seattle Seahawks and New England Patriots – was one of the most dramatic in NFL history. Here is how the battle for the Vince Lombardi Trophy unfolded on a memorable night in the Arizona desert.

NEW ENGLAND 7-0 SEATTLE
It's first blood to New England as Tom Brady – chasing a record-tying fourth Super Bowl win – fires an 11-yard touchdown pass to wide receiver Brandon LaFell.

NEW ENGLAND 7-7 SEATTLE
The Seahawks strike back early in the second quarter as 'Beast Mode' running back Marshawn Lynch rumbles into the end zone on a 3-yard run.

NEW ENGLAND 14-7 SEATTLE
Brady begins to find his groove and moves the Patriots in front with 31 seconds left in the first half as he arrows a 22-yard touchdown pass to tight end Rob Gronkowski.

NEW ENGLAND 14-14 SEATTLE
But Brady leaves just enough time on the clock for Russell Wilson to throw a game-tying 11-yard touchdown pass to Chris Matthews with two seconds remaining in the first half.

NEW ENGLAND 14-24 SEATTLE
After adding a Steven Hauschka field goal and keeping Brady in check with strong defence, the Seahawks open up a 10-point third quarter lead with Wilson's 3-yard pass to Doug Baldwin.

NEW ENGLAND 21-24 SEATTLE
You can't keep a good man down for long and Brady brings the Patriots storming back with a 4-yard touchdown pass to Danny Amendola in the fourth and final period.

NEW ENGLAND 28-24 SEATTLE
The Patriots are in front with 2.02 to play as Brady fires his fourth touchdown pass of the night with this one covering 3 yards to Julian Edelman.

THE MIRACLE CATCH
The Seahawks still have time to grab back the lead and move down to the New England 5-yard line after Jermaine Kearse makes a miracle 33-yard catch from Russell Wilson, bobbling the ball four times before securing the reception while lying flat on his back!

THE INTERCEPTION!
Camped at the New England 1-yard line and with the NFL's best running back (Lynch) in the game, the Seahawks ignore a simple running play and Wilson's pass into the end zone is intercepted by Malcolm Butler with just 20 seconds remaining. The shocking play sees the Patriots crowned as Super Bowl champions for the fourth time under the combination of head coach Bill Belichick and quarterback Tom Brady. After the game, shell-shocked Seahawks coach Pete Carroll faces the accusing media and says: "I can take a punch. You never think you'll throw an interception there."

FINAL SCORE: NEW ENGLAND PATRIOTS 28 SEATTLE SEAHAWKS 24

NFL SUPERSTAR

When he entered the NFL in 2012,

all eyes were on Indianapolis Colts quarterback **Andrew Luck.** Not only was he the hottest prospect to come out of college football in a generation, he was also replacing a living legend in Peyton Manning.

Luck has easily handled that pressure – he took over the worst team in the NFL and has guided them to the end-of-season playoffs every year he's been in the league. It's that kind of production that already has Luck labelled as one of the best quarterbacks in the NFL and a future all-time great.

ANDREW LUCK

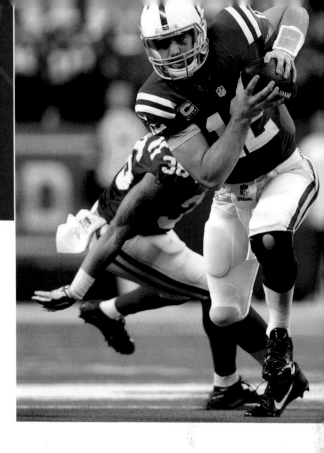

FACT FILE!

Name: Andrew Luck
Date of Birth: September 12, 1989
Position: Quarterback
Team: Indianapolis Colts
NFL Debut: 2012
Honours: 3-time NFL All-Star and holder of 11 NFL records

ON GROWING UP IN LONDON...

"I had a great time. I remember watching quite a few soccer games when I was growing up in St. John's Wood in London. My love of soccer and the Premier League came from my time spent in the UK. That time in my life had a really big impact on my passion for sport."

ON BEING AN NFL QUARTERBACK...

"There's a lot to it. There's a mental and physical side to my position and I certainly have my hands full. It's an interesting position and you deal with a lot of pressure – people seem to care about the quarterback a lot more. I love it and I really enjoy it. I'm very fortunate to be able to play this game."

ON PREPARING FOR GAMES...

"Weekly preparation is probably 75 per cent of playing quarterback. We start on a Monday right after we've played on the Sunday. We look for our mistakes and correct them. Then we begin with a basic overview of the next opponent. We get a general feel for their defence and the game of cat and mouse begins. As the week goes on, our preparation becomes more specialised – Wednesday I might look at third down plays and Thursday will be plays inside their 20-yard line. We break it all down and figure out what's important."

ON NEVER GIVING UP IN GAMES...

"We are coached to never look at the scoreboard, no matter what. You have to play hard from the first whistle until the last whistle, even if you are up by 30 points or down by 50. As a quarterback, you really have to buy into that theory and it can really make a difference at the end of games."

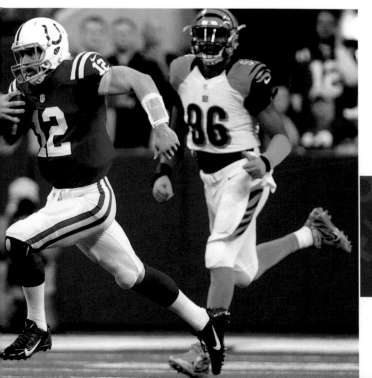

ON GETTING SOME DOWN TIME...

"It's incredibly important to get away from the game. We have a 'no American football' rule after 6pm on a Monday. It's a roller-coaster ride and that's why we only play once per week. You need to take a break from the game to stay sane and healthy. I enjoy reading a lot and I make sure I read every day. I also love watching soccer and playing the FIFA computer game."

DID YOU KNOW?

Andrew Luck's father, Oliver, played quarterback in the NFL for the Houston Oilers from 1982-1986.

WHAT IT FEELS LIKE

Have you ever wondered what it would feel like to be an NFL player? Have you dreamed of that moment when you score the winning touchdown in a Super Bowl or dared to imagine being on the receiving end of a big hit from a ferocious linebacker?

Now you can go onto the field and learn what it feels like when things go right – and wrong – for some of the NFL's biggest stars.

WHAT IT FEELS LIKE TO... GET DRAFTED INTO THE NFL

"It was definitely a dream come true and something I've imagined since I was a young kid, playing American football at the age of six or seven. To have that dream of playing in the NFL become a reality was pretty special." – *Jacksonville Jaguars quarterback, Blake Bortles*

WHAT IT FEELS LIKE TO... BE AN NFL QUARTERBACK

"People really pay attention to what you do and say. To be a quarterback for the 49ers is a great honour. There are great expectations – as the quarterback you need to play well and be that leader and playmaker." – *San Francisco 49ers quarterback, Colin Kaepernick*

WHAT IT FEELS LIKE TO... RUN OVER A DEFENDER

"You feel really excited and good about yourself because the other guy wasn't able to tackle you on that play. I always enjoy running over a defender. I love the physical part of the game and love dishing out big hits to defenders." – *Miami Dolphins running back, Jay Ajayi*

WHAT IT FEELS LIKE TO... BE ON THE RECEIVING END OF A BIG HIT

"It's never a good thing. It tests your toughness but you have to be able to shake it off and come back and make a play. My coach always says, 'Rub some dirt on it, get up and get back in the huddle.' You never want to show any weakness and want to appear as strong as possible."
– *Miami Dolphins wide receiver, Jarvis Landry*

WHAT IT FEELS LIKE TO... SACK THE QUARTERBACK

"It's such a great feeling because it's the culmination of so much hard work and so much practice. You need to have a little bit of luck as well, so any time you can get back there, it's so much fun. I like making NFL quarterbacks uncomfortable."
– *Houston Texans defensive end, J.J. Watt*

WHAT IT FEELS LIKE TO... GIVE UP A QUARTERBACK SACK

"It's demoralising. The other team are celebrating and your quarterback is down and probably not feeling too good and you know it's your fault. That hurts."
– *New York Jets center, Nick Mangold*

WHAT IT FEELS LIKE TO... THROW A WINNING TOUCHDOWN AT THE SUPER BOWL

"That's every kid's dream. You're aware of the magnitude of the occasion but you're not thinking about this being the biggest moment of your career – you're just trying to play. That last throw to Santonio Holmes in Super Bowl XLIII (43) was a blur at the time but, looking back on it, that was a great memory."
– *Pittsburgh Steelers quarterback, Ben Roethlisberger.*

WHAT IT FEELS LIKE TO... WIN A SUPER BOWL

"You think you're going to feel this crazy emotion but when that clock hits zero, you're feeling numb. I knew I had finally done something that set me apart from so many guys who had played this game. If you've won a Super Bowl, you're in an elite category with a very special group of players. It's a numbing feeling."
– *Miami Dolphins wide receiver, Greg Jennings*

WHAT IT FEELS LIKE TO... SCORE A TOUCHDOWN

"It's the best feeling. You work hard and put in so much time each and every week to prepare for a game so to go out and score a touchdown and to hear the crowd cheering, there's no better feeling."
– *Miami Dolphins quarterback, Ryan Tannehill*

FLYING THE FLAG FOR BRITAIN!

The NFL may be as American as the Statue of Liberty or the stars and stripes flag, but that fact is not stopping a growing number of British players from making an impact at the sport's highest level.

MENELIK WATSON

FACT FILE...
Name: Menelik Watson
Date of Birth: December 22, 1988
Position: Offensive Tackle
Team: Oakland Raiders
NFL Debut: 2013

THE LOWDOWN...
Menelik Watson was born and raised in Manchester before heading to America as a teenager to play basketball. He switched to American football and starred at Florida State University before being drafted by the Raiders, where he currently starts on their offensive line.

MENELIK SAYS...
"It's been a great journey so far but there's a lot more to come. I'm trying to b the best. I'm trying to be elite. I just don' have any quit in me."

DID YOU KNOW?
Menelik is a massive Manchester City fan. He played soccer growing up and dreamed of playing in an F.A. Cup Final a Wembley Stadium.

JAY AJAYI

FACT FILE...
Name: Jay Ajayi
Date of Birth: June 15, 1993
Position: Running Back
Team: Miami Dolphins
NFL Debut: 2015

THE LOWDOWN...
Jay Ajayi was born in London and raised in Essex before moving to America at the age of seven. The powerful running back grabbed the attention of NFL teams by scoring 50 touchdowns at Boise State University. He was selected by the Miami Dolphins in the 2015 NFL Draft.

JAY SAYS...
"Knowing I am one of the faces of American football in the UK fires me up and I cannot wait to show the world there is talent over here."

DID YOU KNOW?
Jay is a proud and passionate Arsenal fan and his favourite player when growing up in England was Thierry Henry.

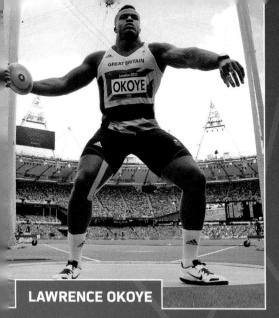

THE LOWDOWN...

Lawrence Okoye has made the high-profile switch from discus finalist at the 2012 London Olympics to budding American football star. Despite learning the sport from scratch, Okoye has turned heads in America with his outstanding athletic skills.

LAWRENCE SAYS...

"As the NFL continues to progress internationally I think we will see more guys doing what I am doing. This is a sign of things to come."

DID YOU KNOW?

Lawrence is a multi-talented sportsman. He was a junior rugby star at London Irish and is fast for a big man, recording a time of 10.95 seconds in the 100 metres.

LAWRENCE OKOYE

FACT FILE...

Name:	Lawrence Okoye
Date of Birth:	October 6, 1991
Position:	Defensive End
Team:	San Francisco 49ers
NFL Debut:	2013

JACK CRAWFORD

FACT FILE...

Name:	Jack Crawford
Date of Birth:	September 7, 1988
Position:	Defensive End
Team:	Dallas Cowboys
NFL Debut:	2012

THE LOWDOWN...

Like Menelik Watson, Jack Crawford travelled to America as a teenage basketball player. The Londoner switched to American football and starred at Penn State University before making his NFL debut with the Oakland Raiders. He is now growing into a key defender for the Dallas Cowboys.

JACK SAYS...

"The NFL fan base in the UK is amazing. They are so into the sport and playing in front of them at Wembley Stadium in 2014 was an experience I will never forget."

DID YOU KNOW...

When he is not playing American football, Jack enjoys producing music.

EFE OBADA

FACT FILE...

Name:	Efe Obada
Date of Birth:	April 13, 1992
Position:	Defensive End
Team:	Dallas Cowboys
NFL Debut:	2015

THE LOWDOWN...

Efe Obada is proof that sporting dreams can come true if you work hard enough. The Londoner played just five games as an amateur for the London Warriors in the British league but was spotted by one of the biggest clubs in America – the Dallas Cowboys.

EFE SAYS...

"This is a dream. It's amazing and life-changing. This is a major turning point in my life and feels like a movie. This is unreal – this doesn't happen to people like me."

DID YOU KNOW...

Efe was working as a warehouse storeman in Hertfordshire before being offered a shot at his NFL dream by the Cowboys.

NFL
SUPERSTAR

It's supposed to be difficult for young players when they move from the amateur ranks of college football into the NFL. Somebody forgot to tell **Odell Beckham Jr.** that was the case as he burst onto the scene and made a sensational impact with the New York Giants in 2014.

Beckham is the hottest property in American football. He already holds dozens of league records, has made arguably the greatest catch in NFL history and is the latest cover boy for the Madden NFL computer game. It's very early in his career, but greatness beckons.

ODELL BECKHAM JR.

FACT FILE!

Name:	Odell Beckham Jr.
Date of Birth:	November 5, 1992
Position:	Wide Receiver
Team:	New York Giants
NFL Debut:	2014
Nickname:	OBJ
Honours:	NFL Rookie of the Year 2014, NFL All-Star and holder of 34 NFL records.

ON MAKING SPECTACULAR CATCHES...

"I practice every day to make the most ridiculous catches I could possibly make – high, low, in front of me or behind. You make those catches in practice so when they come up in games, you're ready. I don't make one-handed catches to show off – I make them when I need to because it's possible to reach further when you're just stretching out one arm."

ON PLAYING FOR THE NEW YORK GIANTS...

"The Giants are a classy team with a great history. I can't even put into words how I felt when the Giants called me on Draft Day to tell me I was about to become a part of their team. That was an experience I will never forget. We are a championship team and we'll be back."

ON APPRECIATING EVERY GAME IN THE NFL...

"Every time I get into the locker room on gameday I look at my helmet and shirt and really cherish that moment. You never know when it could be your last game in the NFL. When I step out on that field, I always think, 'If this is your last game, how do you want to be remembered?'"

ON HOW HE WOULD LIKE TO BE REMEMBERED WHEN HE RETIRES...

"I want to be remembered the same way people think about Jerry Rice – he was the greatest of all time and the best of the best. I want to leave a legacy where people are saying I was the best ever. I strive to be the best of the best."

DID YOU KNOW?

On January 29, 2015, OBJ teamed with New Orleans Saints quarterback Drew Brees to set a new world record. Beckham made 33 one-handed catches in 60 seconds, shattering the previous mark of 10.

NFL AT WEMBLEY WORDSEARCH

By the end of the 2015 season, 20 of the NFL's 32 teams will have played a regular season game at Wembley Stadium.

It's time to grab a pen and go searching for the teams who have graced the hallowed turf in London. The team nicknames are hidden within the wordsearch horizontally and vertically, forwards and backwards, and diagonally. Happy hunting!
(Answers on p60.)

Find the words in the grid.

Words can go horizontally, vertically and diagonally in all eight directions.

```
P  J  L  V  R  S  T  E  E  L  E  R  S  T  T  D
L  H  A  Q  B  M  X  N  D  C  H  L  R  B  G  N
K  F  P  G  W  A  Y  Y  H  T  I  S  E  T  B  J
B  M  J  D  U  R  N  A  C  O  M  N  9  D  U  Y
V  T  E  Y  G  A  R  S  N  Y  K  I  4  V  C  K
I  F  T  M  G  G  R  S  K  T  B  H  L  Z  C  L
K  T  S  B  E  A  P  S  L  K  V  P  X  Z  A  M
I  M  F  R  E  G  I  A  N  T  S  L  K  F  N  Y
N  W  S  B  L  N  S  B  G  C  R  O  B  T  E  M
G  T  T  X  K  N  M  S  R  S  L  D  L  J  E  Y
S  J  T  Q  O  S  L  J  R  O  Y  Q  N  W  R  R
M  Q  K  C  T  K  G  Q  D  E  N  O  R  N  S  M
P  N  L  N  B  I  L  L  S  T  D  C  B  L  M  Y
J  A  I  C  N  Q  J  H  M  L  N  I  O  W  Q  C
F  A  Y  T  S  T  O  I  R  T  A  P  A  S  O  R
S  P  J  S  F  E  I  H  C  X  R  L  H  R  G  C
```

49ERS	COWBOYS	PATRIOTS
BEARS	DOLPHINS	RAIDERS
BILLS	FALCONS	RAMS
BRONCOS	GIANTS	SAINTS
BUCCANEERS	JAGUARS	STEELERS
CHARGERS	JETS	VIKINGS
CHIEFS	LIONS	

TRUE
OR FALSE?

Let's imagine you're an NFL General Manager and you're looking to build your team for the upcoming season. You're sitting down with a key player you hope to sign and one of your big tasks is to find out when he's telling the truth and when he's lying through his teeth. **Can you trust him in a big game?**

Finding out about the character of your players is a key requirement of an NFL General Manager. So let's see if you've got what it takes. Read the 10 facts below and simply work out which ones are true and which ones are massive NFL lies. *(Answers on p60.)*

1. **T F** If you signed up for Green Bay Packers season tickets today, it would take you 955 years to get to the top of the waiting list and receive your tickets.

2. **T F** New York Giants wide receiver Odell Beckham Jr. is the cousin of former England soccer legend David Beckham.

3. **T F** The Cleveland Browns are the only NFL team without a logo on their helmets.

4. **T F** New Orleans Saints head coach Sean Payton played one season as quarterback for the British League's Leicester Panthers.

5. **T F** Indianapolis Colts quarterback Andrew Luck played youth team football for Chelsea while growing up in London.

6. **T F** A real-life lion leads the Detroit Lions out of the tunnel at each of their home games.

7. **T F** A real-life hawk leads the Seattle Seahawks out of the tunnel at each of their home games.

8. **T F** Dallas Cowboys quarterback Tony Romo is an excellent golfer and has played in qualifying tournaments for the U.S. Open.

9. **T F** Baltimore Ravens wide receiver Steve Smith is a massive Manchester United fan.

10. **T F** Wembley Stadium will host the 50th Super Bowl on February 7, 2016.

BEST IN THE BUSINESS...

Just like millions of men, women and children around the world, NFL players are massive fans of American football and when they're not playing, they can often be found watching other games from around the league.

So we grabbed some of the biggest stars of the NFL to ask them which players they rate at their respective positions.

ANTONIO BROWN

ODELL BECKHAM JR – WIDE RECEIVER, NEW YORK GIANTS
Antonio Brown – Wide Receiver, Pittsburgh Steelers
"Antonio Brown is one of those guys I love to watch. I watch receivers like him on film and try to find some things that he does that I can add to my game. He is one of the best."

BEN ROETHLISBERGER – QUARTERBACK, PITTSBURGH STEELERS
Tom Brady – Quarterback, New England Patriots
"I would have to say Tom Brady because he has the most championships and, to me, that's what makes the great ones. There are a lot of great quarterbacks in the NFL like Aaron Rodgers, Peyton Manning and Drew Brees, but Tom has the most championships."

NDAMUKONG SUH – DEFENSIVE TACKLE, MIAMI DOLPHINS
Calais Campbell – Defensive End, Arizona Cardinals
"I have great respect for Houston Texans defensive end J.J. Watt but another guy I really like who is kind of an unsung hero is Calais Campbell, of the Arizona Cardinals. He has always been consistent and he definitely carries a big chunk of that team's defence."

BLAKE BORTLES – QUARTERBACK, JACKSONVILLE JAGUARS
Tom Brady – Quarterback, New England Patriots
"Everybody wants to be like Tom Brady, so of course I want to be like Tom Brady. He's definitely somebody you want to model your game on. He is at the top of his game right now and I can learn a lot from him."

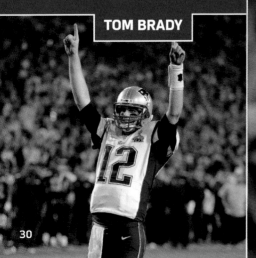

TOM BRADY

CALAIS CAMPBELL

CALVIN JOHNSON

GOLDEN TATE -
WIDE RECEIVER, DETROIT LIONS
Calvin Johnson -
Wide Receiver, Detroit Lions
"Calvin is one of the best to ever play the game. He works hard and is a tremendous leader. Being around Calvin is a real treat. I love trying to keep up with him because he's a workhorse and he makes me a better player."

GREG JENNINGS -
WIDE RECEIVER, MIAMI DOLPHINS
Dez Bryant -
Wide Receiver, Dallas Cowboys
"I really like to watch Dez Bryant. I love the way he goes about playing the game – he attacks the ball, he's physical and he runs well after the catch. He does everything right but there are times when he is so passionate and emotional that it gets the better of him. But he is a special player to watch."

DEZ BRYANT

CALVIN JOHNSON -
WIDE RECEIVER, DETROIT LIONS
Antonio Brown -
Wide Receiver, Pittsburgh Steelers
"There are so many good ones around the league and Dez Bryant is one of those at the top of his game. But I really find it fun to watch my man Antonio Brown. He is quick and shifty and can make a lot of plays out of nothing."

JAY AJAYI -
RUNNING BACK, MIAMI DOLPHINS
Marshawn Lynch -
Running Back, Seattle Seahawks
"I really look up to a guy like Marshawn Lynch because of how he runs the football and fights for every yard. He really is at the top of our game and I strive to be like him."

MARSHAWN LYNCH

NFL FUNNIES

The **NFL is very serious business** with players fighting for all-important wins every weekend. But every now and then, this great sport offers up chances to have a good laugh!

"Look coach, I'm keeping my eye on the ball!"

"Come on, Earl, skipping is fun!"

"To be fair, I don't think there are enough overhead kicks in the NFL."

"You're right... this grass smells great."

"So is there chewing gum on the bottom of my shoe or not?"

"This seemed like a good idea when I started it!"

"And if you need to go to the toilet, just put your hand up."

"Hey! I didn't sign up for the ice bucket challenge!"

"These really are great seats... now pass me some popcorn!"

NFL SUPERSTAR

Even though he is in just his fourth NFL season, Seattle Seahawks quarterback **Russell Wilson** has already proven himself to be one of the best in the league, guiding his team to appearances in the last two Super Bowls.

Wilson led the Seahawks to NFL title success after the 2013 season and proved that size is not everything in American football. At 5-foot-11, Wilson became the shortest quarterback in league history to win a Super Bowl. The sky is the limit and the future is bright for this young star.

RUSSELL WILSON

FACT FILE!

Name: Russell Wilson

Date of Birth: November 29, 1988

Position: Quarterback

Team: Seattle Seahawks

NFL Debut: 2012

Nickname: Dange-Russ

Honours: 2-time NFL all-star

ON BEING A ROLE MODEL FOR YOUNG FANS...

"I keep my focus on being a role model. I'm gifted to be in this position to hopefully influence people in a positive way. I want to help make a difference in everybody's life. I try to have a positive atmosphere around me and I try to influence as many kids as I can and try to get involved in the community as much as I can. I also want to be a great team-mate."

ON HIS NFL HEROES...

"New Orleans Saints quarterback Drew Brees was a guy I looked up to ever since my dad told me about him back in middle school and high school. He said, 'Hey, you have to watch this guy.' When I was playing college football at Wisconsin, I watched every single throw he made in the NFL – I studied his craft and studied his game. He's just a great inspiration. He does things right, he's a great leader and he's so poised in big situations."

ON BEING DRIVEN BY LAST YEAR'S SUPER BOWL LOSS TO NEW ENGLAND...

"I think it's a motivating factor, for sure. But I don't think it's the ultimate one. I think when you're an ultimate competitor, it comes down to wanting to go out there and dominating as much as we can in every game. That's just our mind-set. So win or lose, we overcome things and we're used to that. Our personalities, our experiences as young men, every guy can find something they've overcome. That's our mentality."

ON HOW HE WOULD LIKE TO BE REMEMBERED...

"In terms of my legacy on the field, I want to be considered a winner. The goal of playing quarterback is win, win, win. That's all that really matters at the end of the day. Off the field, I want to be a Christian man who helps lead, helps change lives and helps serve other people. It's not about me, you know? It's about helping other people."

BUILD YOUR OWN NFL TEAM!

Have you ever wanted to run your own NFL team? Well, now you can. We're giving you the chance to build your very own American football club. You can name your new NFL team, design their uniform and helmet and pick some star players from around the league to get you started.

Then all you need to do is go out and win some games!

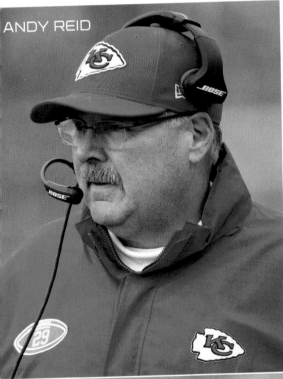

ANDY REID

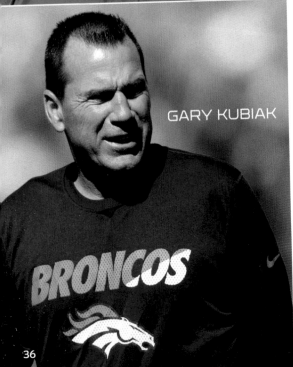

GARY KUBIAK

PICK YOUR HEAD COACH

Who do you want to head up your team? A former player who can identify with his athletes, a master tactician who can out-think the opposition or a fiery fist-pumper who motivates his men?

Former players
Jason Garrett – Dallas Cowboys
Ron Rivera – Carolina Panthers
Gary Kubiak – Denver Broncos

Master tacticians
Andy Reid – Kansas City Chiefs
Bill Belichick – New England Patriots
Chip Kelly – Philadelphia Eagles

Man motivators
Rex Ryan – Buffalo Bills
Gus Bradley – Jacksonville Jaguars
Jim Tomsula – San Francisco 49ers

PICK YOUR QUARTERBACK

Who is going to be firing the passes for your team? Are you opting for a wily veteran who has been there and done it, an exciting young gun or a quarterback who can run and pass with equal skill?

Proven veterans
Peyton Manning – Denver Broncos
Aaron Rodgers – Green Bay Packers
Tom Brady – New England Patriots

Young stars
Andrew Luck – Indianapolis Colts
Ryan Tannehill – Miami Dolphins
Colin Kaepernick – San Francisco 49ers

Dual threats
Cam Newton – Carolina Panthers
Russell Wilson – Seattle Seahawks
Robert Griffin III – Washington Redskins

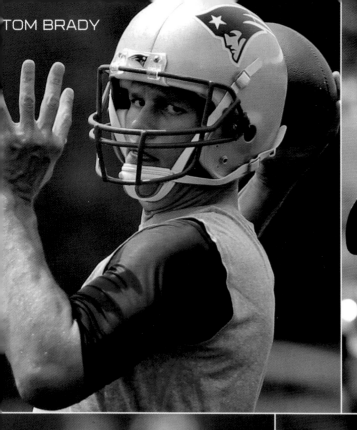
TOM BRADY

RYAN TANNEHILL

PEYTON MANNING

ANDREW LUCK

ROBERT GRIFFIN III

AARON RODGERS

LUKE KUECHLY

PICK YOUR STAR DEFENDER

You've picked your coach and the leading players to help you score points – now it's time to find somebody to slow down the opposition. Do you want a man-mountain on your defensive line, a versatile linebacker or somebody who can cover the quickest receivers in the game?

Big defensive linemen
J.J. Watt – Houston Texans
Ndamukong Suh – Miami Dolphins
Gerald McCoy – Tampa Bay Buccaneers

Explosive linebackers
Luke Kuechly – Carolina Panthers
Von Miller – Denver Broncos
Justin Houston – Kansas City Chiefs

Play-making defensive backs
Darrelle Revis – New York Jets
Richard Sherman – Seattle Seahawks
Earl Thomas – Seattle Seahawks

PICK YOUR SKILL POSITION STAR

It's time to find another player who can help your attack and turn your quarterback into a star. But do you want a game-breaking wide receiver, a reliable running back or a tight end who can create problems for the defence?

The runners
Jamaal Charles – Kansas City Chiefs
Le'Veon Bell – Pittsburgh Steelers
Marshawn Lynch – Seattle Seahawks

The receivers
Dez Bryant – Dallas Cowboys
Calvin Johnson – Detroit Lions
Antonio Brown – Pittsburgh Steelers

The tight ends
Jason Witten – Dallas Cowboys
Rob Gronkowski – New England Patriots
Jimmy Graham – Seattle Seahawks

DEZ BRYANT

TEAM NAME _____

HEAD COACH _____

QUARTERBACK _____

SKILL POSITION STAR _____

STAR DEFENDER _____

Design your own team uniform!

You need to start with a team badge or logo. Then pick your team colours (usually no more than two main colours), and maybe some extra graphics like stripes or stars that can add detail and style to your team's look.

NFL SUPERSTAR

When Aaron Rodgers replaced the legendary Brett Favre as the Green Bay Packers full-time starting quarterback in 2008, some fans were nervous. They knew Rodgers had potential, but Favre was one of the greatest players in NFL history. Was the young star capable of filling such big shoes?

There was no need to worry. Rodgers has been fantastic. He's already won a Super Bowl and been named Most Valuable Player in that game, he's a two-time NFL MVP and is currently ranked as the highest-rated quarterback in league history. For many, Rodgers is the gold standard when it comes to today's NFL quarterbacks.

AARON RODGERS

FACT FILE!

Name: Aaron Rodgers
Date of Birth: December 2, 1983
Position: Quarterback
Team: Green Bay Packers
NFL Debut: 2005
Honours: 4-time NFL All-Star, Super Bowl 45 MVP, 2-time NFL MVP

ON LIFE AS AN NFL QUARTERBACK...

"There's a lot of pressure and expectation that goes with being an NFL quarterback. We get too much of the credit when our team is playing well and too much of the blame when we're losing. But it's exciting – I always wanted to be a quarterback and I'm living out a childhood dream."

ON PLAYING FOR THE GREEN BAY PACKERS...

"Growing up as a sports fan you know what kind of organisation the Packers are and you understand their history of winning and the legends who have played here. Then when you join the team, you realise it goes much deeper than that – the Packers are a community-based team and the only club in American sports without a true owner. Our fans own the team and it's a very special place to play."

ON WINNING THE SUPER BOWL...

"It does take some pressure off. At the same time, the bar has been raised and we are expected to go to the Super Bowl and win it every year. But that's okay – that's what I want to do. That's the kind of success I dreamed of so why not go and get a couple more? We have the guys in place and that's our goal every year."

ON HAVING FUN WHILE PLAYING IN THE NFL...

"The best thing is that this never really feels like a job. We're playing a game we love and getting paid very well to do it. I don't take myself too seriously. I grow a moustache every year during training camp because I enjoy funny facial hair and I like to let my personality come out. It's goofy at times and I can be dry with my humour, but I just like to have a good time. As a leader, you have to be yourself."

DID YOU KNOW?

In his spare time, Rodgers enjoys playing golf and video games, as well as playing musical instruments such as the guitar and the piano.

THE FEARSOME FIVE!

The NFL has become renowned for high-scoring games filled with breath-taking touchdowns. But even though scoring points is at an all-time high, there are still some outstanding defenders hell-bent on making life difficult for offenses around the league.

Let's hear from five of the NFL's leading defenders on their life on the other side of the ball.

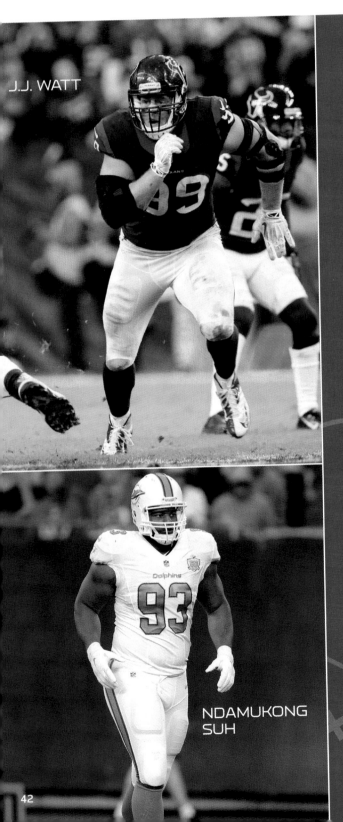

J.J. WATT

NDAMUKONG SUH

J.J. WATT -
DEFENSIVE END, HOUSTON TEXANS

J.J. Watt is a dominating presence on the Houston defence who is routinely voted as one of the very best defenders in the league. He can also play some offense, scoring five touchdowns last season.

Watt says: "If it's a quarterback's league, somebody has to go and chase the quarterback and I guess that's me. I just do my best every day to go out there and get after them and see what I can do to make them uncomfortable."

NDAMUKONG SUH -
DEFENSIVE TACKLE, MIAMI DOLPHINS

Away from the gridiron, Ndamukong Suh is one of the nicest guys you could ever wish to meet. On the pitch, he is a terror and one of the meanest, toughest and most intimidating defenders in the NFL.

Suh says: "I'm in a position where I can affect the passing game, either by getting sacks or freeing up the guy next to me. It's exciting. Offenses are finding ways to be better but I'm glad I'm on the side of the ball that has the uphill battle of trying to stop the machines that are being created."

LUKE KUECHLY -
LINEBACKER, CAROLINA PANTHERS

Off the field, Luke Kuechly looks a bit like Clark Kent with his perfectly-styled hair and glasses. On the pitch, he turns into Superman and is a fast and hard-hitting tackling machine who has become a star.

Kuechly says: "My advice to anyone in sports is be nice to everyone because that's the right way to do it. I'm always trying to get better and if you don't do that, you're just wasted as a player."

RICHARD SHERMAN -
CORNERBACK, SEATTLE SEAHAWKS

This former college wide receiver is one of the most confident and brashest players in the NFL today. But he backs up his words with outstanding play and challenges Revis as the league's best cornerback.

Sherman says: "I'm the best in the game. There is a very common misconception about me. Some believe I lack respect, especially for my opponents. This couldn't be further from the truth. There are few things I enjoy more than watching tape and breaking down quarterbacks."

DARRELLE REVIS -
CORNERBACK, NEW YORK JETS

The New York Jets cornerback has long been considered one of the best defenders of the pass in the NFL. Revis is an all-time great with smooth, technically perfect skills and sprinter's speed.

Revis says: "There is a lot of pressure that comes with playing cornerback in the NFL. I liken it to a two-on-one fast break in basketball – it is the quarterback and the receiver against me. It's always a two-on-one situation but I love it and I love to play this game."

RICHARD SHERMAN

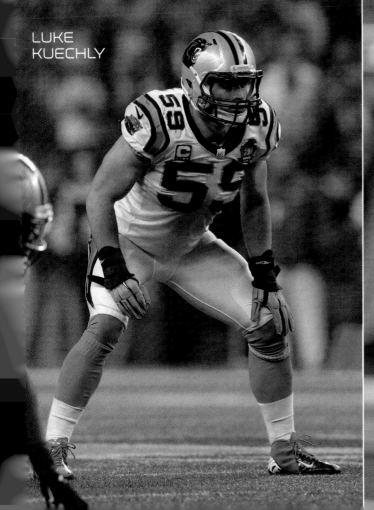

LUKE KUECHLY

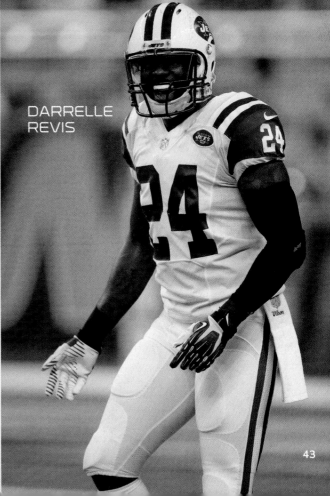

DARRELLE REVIS

NFL SUPERSTAR

The NFL is full of giant men capable of running fast, hitting hard and wowing the fans with outstanding displays of athleticism. But few can match the amazing achievements of Houston Texans defensive end **J.J. Watt** and that's why he's one of the league's true superstars.

This man mountain can leave the best NFL quarterbacks shaking in their boots. But he can also run like the wind and score touchdowns when he makes occasional appearances on offense. The hard-working, talented and often scary defender can simply do it all!

J.J. WATT

FACT FILE!

Name: J.J. WATT
Date of Birth: March 22, 1989
Position: Defensive End
Team: Houston Texans
NFL Debut: 2011
Honours: 3-time NFL All-Star and two-time NFL Defensive Player of the Year

ON BEING A HARD WORKER...

"You're always trying to get better and trying to improve. You never know how you're going to perform but all I can do is try to be the best player I can be every single day. All I do is go out there and try to make my team-mates proud, try to make our fans proud and then just be the best player that I can be. Hard work, dedication and sacrifice makes you great."

ON BEING TOLD HE WAS TOO SMALL TO PLAY AMERICAN FOOTBALL...

"People told me in high school that I was too small to play American football and I'm still playing so I'm happy. That tells people that you should believe in yourself and be willing to have big dreams. But you also have to be willing to work for them and make sacrifices. And then if you want something, go and get it – don't let anybody tell you that you can't or that you shouldn't."

ON EARNING HIS BIG $100 MILLION CONTRACT...

"When you get that big contract you want to show people that you earned it. Being a fan of sports, I see people getting big contracts all the time. And as a fan, what you want to see is that player go out there and earn that contract and show that they deserve it. Every single day I'm trying to do everything I can on that front."

ON HIS FAVOURITE QUARTERBACK TO SACK IN THE NFL...

"It doesn't matter to me who I sack, as long as I get them. I'll take whoever is next up!"

DID YOU KNOW?

J.J. Watt is a massive Chelsea fan and lists Didier Drogba and Frank Lampard among his favourite all-time players.

MY FAVOURITE NFL STADIUM

Every NFL star loves playing in front of his home fans. But with so many spectacular stadiums across the United States of America, away games can also prove to be very memorable.

Let's find out which stadium – outside of their own – the stars of the NFL enjoy playing in.

BLAKE BORTLES –
Quarterback, Jacksonville Jaguars

WEMBLEY STADIUM - home of the NFL's International Series games

"London was awesome when I played there for the first time so I would have to say Wembley Stadium. That was definitely an unparalleled environment. It was a cool atmosphere to play in and I'm excited to go back."

GREG JENNINGS –
Wide Receiver, Miami Dolphins

LAMBEAU FIELD – home of the Green Bay Packers

"There's nothing like Lambeau Field - you feel the presence of the guys who played before you. I can go on and on about how special that place is and how great the fan base is in Green Bay. Just walking out of the tunnel in that stadium is a special and emotional experience - it has to be Lambeau Field."

PAUL WORRILOW –
Linebacker, Atlanta Falcons

LAMBEAU FIELD – home of the Green Bay Packers

"I would have to say Lambeau Field. That was a really good stadium to play in when I played up there against the Packers during the 2013 season. There is just so much history associated with that stadium in Green Bay and it would have to be my favourite in the NFL outside of Atlanta."

JORDAN CAMERON –
Tight End, Miami Dolphins

HEINZ FIELD – home of the Pittsburgh Steelers

"I like playing at Heinz Field in Pittsburgh. They do a pretty good job of getting that crowd riled up. They play this song 'Renegade' at a big moment, normally in the fourth quarter, and the crowd goes insane. Everyone is waving the Terrible Towel and it's a cool moment and a special place to play."

NDAMUKONG SUH –
Defensive Tackle, Miami Dolphins

AT&T STADIUM – home of the Dallas Cowboys

"I would have to say Dallas because I have gone there many times in the pros. I haven't always come out on the winning side but I've enjoyed the experience. When you walk out the tunnel in Dallas you go through a bar and fans are yelling and screaming and heckling you, but that creates a great atmosphere and that's what it comes down to as a player – you want to play in that kind of atmosphere."

NFL QUIZ

1. Which team has won the most Super Bowls with six?

_____

2. Star quarterback Peyton Manning spent 12 seasons with which team before joining the Denver Broncos in 2012?

_____

3. Which NFL team celebrates each home touchdown with the 'Lambeau Leap?'

_____

4. Which two NFL teams play in the state of Texas?

_____

5. Five NFL teams have bird nicknames. Can you name them?

_____

6. England and Tottenham striker Harry Kane is a big fan of which NFL team?

_____

7. How many points does your team score if you are awarded a safety?

_____

8. Eli Manning is a two-time Super Bowl-winning quarterback for which NFL club?

_____

9. Which NFL team plays its home games at Arrowhead Stadium?

_____

10. Which of these teams does not play in black shirts...Pittsburgh Steelers, Detroit Lions or Oakland Raiders?

_____

Can you name these five NFL teams by taking a look at their helmet logos?

1

2

3

4

5

NFL ANAGRAMS

We're all mixed up and need your help! Unscramble the anagrams to reveal the names of five NFL teams...

Koala sand rider **NO STUNT HOAXES**
WEASELS COACH BIG EARS
TAKE HATS
IMPISH MAD LION _____

_____
_____
_____
_____
_____

And now prove you're an NFL champion by unscrambling these words to discover five of the league's star quarterbacks.

BODY TRAM **GROANERS ROAD**
CLAW DUNKER ILL NURSES SLOW
NINETY PONG MAN _____

_____
_____
_____
_____

INSIDE THE LOCKER ROOM

It's time to go behind the scenes and into the world of an American football player as we take you inside the locker room. Let's find out what goes on behind those closed doors before, during and after big games in the NFL.

DURING THE WEEK...

"I'm in there every day. It's important to touch base with your players. There was a time when that was their hidden place where what went on in the locker room stayed in the locker room, but I can't stay out. If I'm going to help players get better, that is going to take me into the locker room and our players understand that." – *Gus Bradley, Head Coach, Jacksonville Jaguars.*

BEFORE THE GAME...

"I like to get a little solitary and then I start getting really, really angry. I wind myself up. It usually ends up with me at the door shouting, 'Let us go' and the PR guy holding us back."
- *Menelik Watson, Offensive Tackle, Oakland Raiders.*

"As soon as I get to my locker, I just sit there for five minutes looking at my jersey and really cherish the moment. I think about what I'm going to do in that game. When I get on the field before the kick-off, I ask myself, 'How do you want to be remembered?'"
– *Odell Beckham Jr., Wide Receiver, New York Giants.*

HALF TIME...

"It's a quick period of time for us – just 12 minutes. You grab a quick snack – either a bar of something or a piece of fruit – and drink some Gatorade. We'll talk about things we like in the game and what we want to get into the plan for the second half. Then the coaches will come in, give us the adjustments they have created and we're back on the field. Before you know it, we're playing again."
– *Ryan Tannehill, Quarterback, Miami Dolphins.*

AFTER THE GAME...

"There is a big contrast between how you feel after a win or a loss in the NFL. The players make sacrifices physically and emotionally because this is a demanding sport. When you lose, you have to try to deal with it but when you win, it's a feeling of total elation and there are not many things better than that."
– *Joe Philbin, Head Coach, Miami Dolphins.*

"Our locker rooms smell really bad after games. You kind of get used to the smell. I'm used to that unique smell of sweat and mud. I'm sure it doesn't smell great to people who have to come into our locker room but to us, after a win, it smells pretty damn good."
– *Aaron Rodgers, Quarterback, Green Bay Packers.*

NFL SUPERSTAR

At 6-foot-5, Detroit Lions wide receiver Calvin Johnson is bigger than most defenders in the NFL and is one of the most physically imposing players on the gridiron.

In a league packed with explosive receivers who make breath-taking catches every weekend, Johnson has long been considered the best of the bunch and is a true NFL superstar and all-round nice guy!

ON USING HIS SIZE TO HIS ADVANTAGE WHEN CATCHING PASSES...

"If you can couple size with speed, it's tough on defenders. And if you have that ability to go up for the ball, it's almost like playing against children sometimes."

CALVIN JOHNSON

FACT FILE!

Name: Calvin Johnson

Date of Birth: September 29, 1985

Position: Wide Receiver

Team: Detroit Lions

NFL Debut: 2007

Nickname: Megatron

Honours: 5-time NFL All-Star and holder of 15 NFL receiving records.

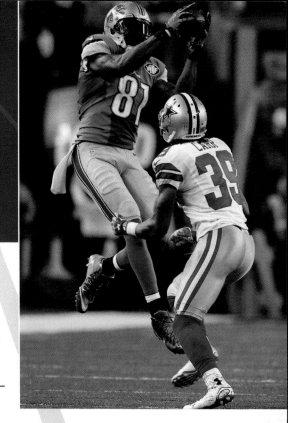

ON LETTING HIS PLAY DO THE TALKING ON THE PITCH...

"After my first year my coach told me, 'You're not coming out of the game.' So I don't have extra energy to spend talking trash to defenders. I've got a game to play and if I'm out there talking, that might take away some of my focus."

ON SPENDING TIME WITH HIS TEAM-MATES...

"I take everybody in. I invite the guys to my house and we have a good time. We spend time together off the field, whether it's playing video games or we have a cook out. I talk to my team-mates all the time and I love my team."

ON HIS MEGATRON NICKNAME...

"It's a great nickname. When I first got to Detroit the Transformers movie had just come out and the number one receiver on the team, Roy Williams, started calling me Megatron. I love it."

ON BEING CONSIDERED AN ALL-TIME NFL GREAT...

"When I get mentioned with the greatest players in NFL history, it's humbling and it just makes me want to work harder. I can't rest – I've got to keep grinding. I have high expectations for myself."

DID YOU KNOW?

Sports scientists have gauged that due to his height, long arms and leaping ability, Calvin Johnson could catch a pass thrown to the top of a basketball backboard.

MATCH THE MASCOT

The NFL is more than just a game -
it is a full-on show in order to entertain the fans in the
stadium. The players are cheered on by the fans in the
stands but also by their team mascot and cheerleaders
on the sidelines.

But how well do you know your entertaining
and glamorous NFL cheering crews?

Simply match each mascot with the cheerleaders of
their NFL team. Good luck! *(Answers on p.61)*

B

A

1

2

C

4

3

E

D

5

A WEEK IN THE LIFE OF AN NFL QUARTERBACK

Quarterbacks are often described as the glamour boys of the NFL but they do have to work hard in order to succeed at one of the toughest and most important positions in any sport.

Being a star quarterback in the NFL requires a lot of dedication and commitment. Every NFL player will spend several days preparing for each weekend's game and the quarterback – as a leader of his team – has to be front and centre on the practice field, in the meeting room and while watching videos of the upcoming opponent late into the night.

So let's find out about life as an NFL quarterback by spending a week with Miami Dolphins star Ryan Tannehill.

MONDAY...
We come into our training facility and watch film of the previous day's game. I will already have watched it on the Sunday night but I watch it again on Monday. Then the remainder of the day is about rest and recovery – we're sitting in the ice tubs, we're stretching and having massages, whatever it takes to get your body ready to go for the next week.

TUESDAY...
On Tuesday we start fully preparing for the next game. There is a lot of film study. I spend a lot of time watching film of games involving the team we're playing next. Then, as quarterbacks, we are given the new plays that go into our playbook that will be used in that weekend's game.

WEDNESDAY...
Wednesday is really when you come back together as a team and the coaching staff will formally present the new plays for the week and give us the game plan for the upcoming opponent. This is the first practice day of the week and Wednesday is usually the heaviest session with the most contact and hitting.

THURSDAY...

It's more of the same. On the practice field, we move from normal downs into more specialised situations. So we will practice the plays we want to run on third down and it is a more specialised session, although we still work on our general approach to the game as well. This tends to be a lighter practice with us just wearing helmets and no shoulder pads.

FRIDAY...

Friday is usually what we call a red zone day, which means we put in the plays we would like to run when we are inside the opponent's 20-yard line and looking to score touchdowns. We do a lot of our throwing practice with seven offensive players against seven defensive guys on days like this and, again, this is a lighter practice in terms of hitting.

SATURDAY...

We come into our training facility in the morning and have meetings to recap everything we have put into our plan during the course of the week. Then we'll have a walk-through practice where we run through the 60-plus plays we plan to use in the game and we'll move downfield at walking pace. It's more mental preparation than anything else. I don't really get anxious before I go to bed on a Saturday night. I've done my preparation throughout the week so I feel confident and ready to go.

SUNDAY... *(before the game)...*

It's gameday! It's an awesome feeling. This is why we prepare all week long and why we train all through the year. You only have 16 regular season opportunities and you try to take advantage of every one of them. It's nothing crazy and I don't have special underwear or lucky socks but I do have a routine on gameday – I like to get to the stadium at the same time, I do things on the field in the same order in terms of my stretching and warm-ups. I stick to that routine.

SUNDAY... *(after the game)...*

There is a huge difference between that feeling of winning or losing in the NFL. There's nothing like an NFL locker room after you've pulled out a tough win. It's great to celebrate with your team-mates. And a loss is obviously terrible and tough to get over. But by Sunday night, you're back on the horse and ready to get going for the next week.

NFL AT WEMBLEY

When NFL games are played each weekend, America comes to a stand-still to watch the action-packed drama unfold – from San Francisco and Seattle on the west coast to cities such as Miami and New York in the east.

But NFL fans now look further afield to follow their favourite sport because American football has ventured across the pond. As a result of the NFL's international growth, a total of 14 regular season games will have been played at London's Wembley Stadium by the end of the 2015 season.

And the passionate and loud British fans are making quite an impact on players and coaches who have been heading to the UK to play in sold out regular season contests since 2007.

Eric Decker – Wide Receiver, New York Jets
Decker played for the Denver Broncos in their 24-16 loss to the San Francisco 49ers in 2010 and returned with the Jets in 2015.

"I played in 2010 with Denver and what an experience that was for me. London is a beautiful city, we played in a great stadium and the fans were ecstatic about American football and you can see how much the sport is growing in the UK. It's nice to get over there and to spread the game."

Bill Belichick – Head Coach, New England Patriots
The four-time Super Bowl-winning coach guided his Patriots to victories in London against Tampa Bay in 2009 and St. Louis in 2012.

"We've had two good experiences over in London. The fans were enthusiastic about the game and it was a great venue. For those of us involved, it was really good to be part of spreading this great game around the world."

Greg Jennings –
Wide Receiver, Miami Dolphins

Jennings starred in the Minnesota Vikings' 34-27 win over the Pittsburgh Steelers in 2013, scoring two touchdowns and returned with the Dolphins in 2015.

"I love London and the fans are great. They epitomise a love of the game. I went off on a long touchdown catch and run early in the game and the crowd went crazy. I really feel like players have to go and experience that atmosphere at Wembley Stadium. Playing in London was far beyond what I expected – it blew my expectations out of the water."

Gus Bradley –
Head Coach, Jacksonville Jaguars

Bradley's Jaguars are playing at least one regular season game in the UK every year from 2013 to 2016.

"It's just been such a great experience for our team. Every aspect has been great – the crowd, the atmosphere and the enthusiasm of the fans. Our players have really embraced the experience. It's great to play in that type of environment. Each year our players go over there and experience more of what the event entails and more and more they buy into it."

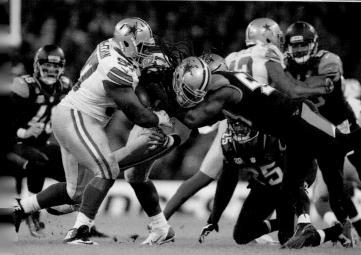

Jason Garrett –
Head Coach, Dallas Cowboys

Garrett's Cowboys played against the Jacksonville Jaguars in 2014 and romped to a 31-17 victory.

"I'll never forget the moment coming out of the tunnel. We've come out of a lot of tunnels but just the visual of looking up and seeing the grand stadium that it is and to experience that atmosphere, it was just unbelievable. Everything about the atmosphere was just something else. It was very memorable. We've got to find a way to keep growing these games."

NFL AT WEMBLEY FACTS...

✓ **The Miami Dolphins have played the most regular** season games at Wembley Stadium (3). The Dolphins played in the first match-up against the New York Giants in 2007 and again in 2014 and 2015.

✓ **New York Giants quarterback Eli Manning** scored the first touchdown in a regular season game played in the UK, finding the end zone on a 10-yard run against Miami in 2007.

✓ **Honorary captains at NFL** games at Wembley Stadium have included Formula 1 ace Lewis Hamilton, England rugby legend Martin Johnson, swimming gold medallist Rebecca Adlington and England and Chelsea stopper John Terry.

✓ **The 2011 game** between the Tampa Bay Buccaneers and Chicago Bears was temporarily halted in the first half when a squirrel ran onto the pitch!

✓ **NFL pre-season games** known as American Bowls were played at the old Wembley Stadium each summer from 1985 to 1993.

QUIZ ANSWERS

WEMBLEY WORDSEARCH, PAGE 28

NFL TRUE OR FALSE, PAGE 29

1. True - Packers have a season ticket waiting list of more than 86,000 and only 90 tickets come available each year.
2. False - There is no family connection between the two Beckhams.
3. True - The Browns helmet is plain orange with a brown and white stripe.
4. True - Sean Payton did indeed play in the UK in the late 1980s.
5. False - Andrew Luck did grow up in London but was never on Chelsea's books.
6. False - Would you want to run out behind a fully-grown lion? Thought not!
7. True - A hawk named 'Taima' leads the Seahawks out at CenturyLink Field.
8. True - Tony Romo once shot a 69 in US Open qualifying.
9. True - Steve Smith is a huge 'Red' and has attended games at Old Trafford.
10. False - Levi's Stadium - home of the San Francisco 49ers - will host Super Bowl 50.

NFL QUIZ, PAGE 48

NFL HELMETS, PAGE 48

MATCH THE MASCOT, PAGES 54-55

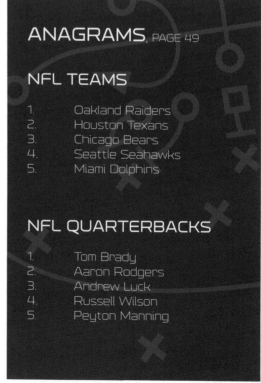

ANAGRAMS, PAGE 49

NFL TEAMS

NFL QUARTERBACKS

WHERE'S UNION JAXSON?

Why would the mascot of the Jacksonville Jaguars "UNION JAXSON" appear at a Green Bay Packers game, and how did he get in without being noticed?

Can you find him?